owya

D1524556

CIVIL WAR SPIES

ESSENTIAL LIBRARY OF
★ THE CIVIL ★
WAR

Essential Library

An Imprint of Abdo Publishing
abdopublishing.com

BY ROBERT GRAYSON

CONTENT CONSULTANT

DR. WILLIAM FEIS
PROFESSOR OF HISTORY
BUENA VISTA UNIVERSITY

abdopublishing.com

Published by Abdo Publishing, a division of ABDO, PO Box 398166, Minneapolis, Minnesota 55439. Copyright © 2017 by Abdo Consulting Group, Inc. International copyrights reserved in all countries. No part of this book may be reproduced in any form without written permission from the publisher. Essential Library™ is a trademark and logo of Abdo Publishing.

Printed in the United States of America, North Mankato, Minnesota

042016
092016

 THIS BOOK CONTAINS
RECYCLED MATERIALS

Cover Photo: Library of Congress
Interior Photos: Library of Congress, 1, 7, 32, 47, 49, 50, 54, 72, 75, 77, 84, 98 (bottom); Everett Historical/Shutterstock Images, 4, 9, 12, 17, 23, 26, 30, 98 (top), 99 (top); North Wind Picture Archives, 14; The Print Collector/Print Collector/Getty Images, 21; Photo Quest/Getty Images, 25; Theodore Russell Davis/Corbis, 36; Kean Collection/Getty Images, 38, 62; Liszt Collection/Heritage Images/Getty Images, 43; Granger Historical Picture Archive, 45, 91; iStockphoto, 57; AS400 DB/Corbis, 60, 64, 87; St. Lawrence University, 67; MPI/Getty Images, 70; Stock Montage/Getty Images, 81, 99 (bottom); Kent Weakley/Shutterstock Images, 93; National Archives, 97

Editor: Kari Cornell
Series Designers: Kelsey Oseid and Maggie Villaume

Cataloging-in-Publication Data

Names: Grayson, Robert, author.
Title: Civil War spies / by Robert Grayson.
Description: Minneapolis, MN : Abdo Publishing, [2017] | Series: Essential library of the Civil War | Includes bibliographical references and index.
Identifiers: LCCN 2015960293 | ISBN 9781680782776 (lib. bdg.) | ISBN 9781680774665 (ebook)
Subjects: LCSH: United States--History--Civil War, 1861-1865--Secret Service--Juvenile literature. | United States--History-- Civil War, 1861-1865--Underground movements--Juvenile literature. | Spies--United States--History--19th century--Juvenile literature. | Spies--Confederate States of America--Juvenile literature.
Classification: DDC 973.7/86--dc23
LC record available at http://lccn.loc.gov/2015960293

CONTENTS

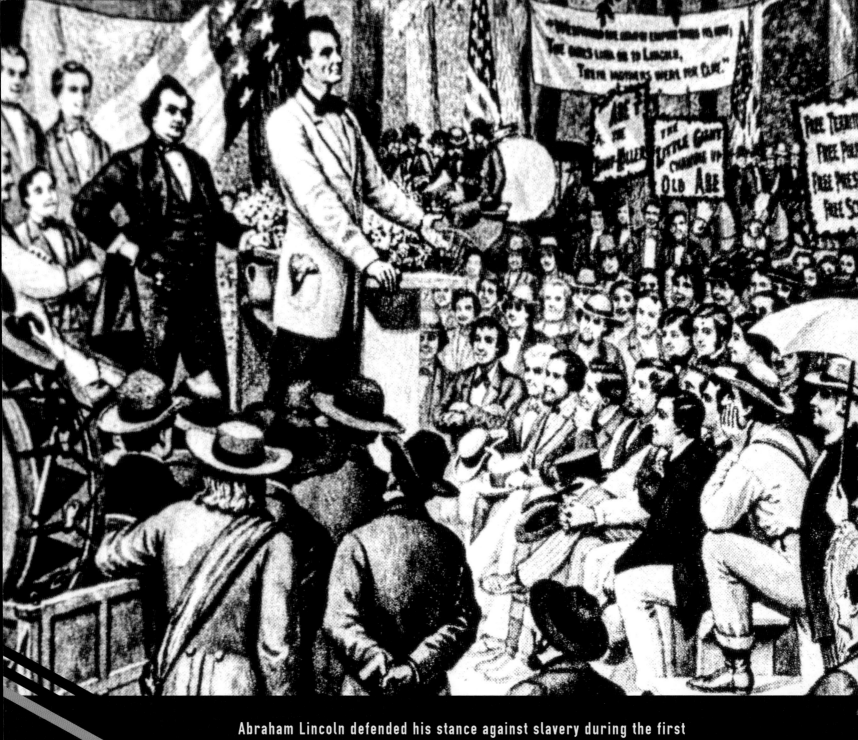

Abraham Lincoln defended his stance against slavery during the first Lincoln-Douglass presidential debate in 1858.

SAVING LINCOLN

Bitterly cold temperatures gripped Philadelphia, Pennsylvania, on January 21, 1861. But the information that Samuel Felton, president of the Philadelphia, Wilmington, and Baltimore Railroad (PW&B), was about to share with a private detective he had just hired was even more chilling. Felton told investigator Allan Pinkerton about rumors, then swirling around the Northeast, of an attack on the railroad. According to the rumors, Southern sympathizers had been planning to blow up key points along the railroad between Wilmington, Delaware, and Baltimore, Maryland. The attacks were being planned in case a war broke out between the North and the South. Destroying PW&B railroad bridges and track would make it difficult for the Northern states making up the Union to quickly move troops and supplies into position to attack the South. These Southern groups had begun plotting on November 6, 1860, the day Abraham Lincoln was elected president of the United States.

At the time, slavery was common throughout the South. Lincoln was against slavery and won the presidency with very little support in the South. As a member of the Republican Party, Lincoln vowed to confine slavery to the Southern states and ban it in any new US territories or states.

Southerners did not trust Lincoln. Southern sympathizers, such as those Felton was concerned about, thought Lincoln would try to abolish slavery throughout the nation, using force if necessary. Southern sympathizers were training to fight a war to maintain the South's way of life. They were learning how to blow up railroad bridges and disrupt rail transport. These rebellious Southerners realized how important the rail lines would be for transporting Northern troops and war supplies.

By the time Felton heard this news, South Carolina had already seceded from the Union on December 20, 1860. Other Southern states, fearing Lincoln might try to abolish slavery, were poised to withdraw as well. Mississippi, Florida, Alabama, Georgia, Louisiana, and Texas seceded from the Union by February 1, 1861. Lincoln was not even sworn into office until March.

In Felton's meeting with Pinkerton, the railroad president told the private detective, "We do know this much. Between Wilmington and Baltimore—and in Baltimore itself—there are many dangerous Southern sympathizers. Can you find out who they are and what they are planning?"[1] With a stern resolve, Pinkerton, who had investigated many crimes against railway lines in the past, said he would start his investigation immediately. But even this hardened detective was not prepared for what he was about to discover.

The burly Pinkerton was quite familiar with Lincoln. In 1855, Pinkerton, then a detective in Chicago, Illinois, was hired by the Illinois Central Railroad to investigate a rash of robberies and other crimes along the train line's Midwestern route. The attorney who drew up the contract between the railroad and Pinkerton was Lincoln.

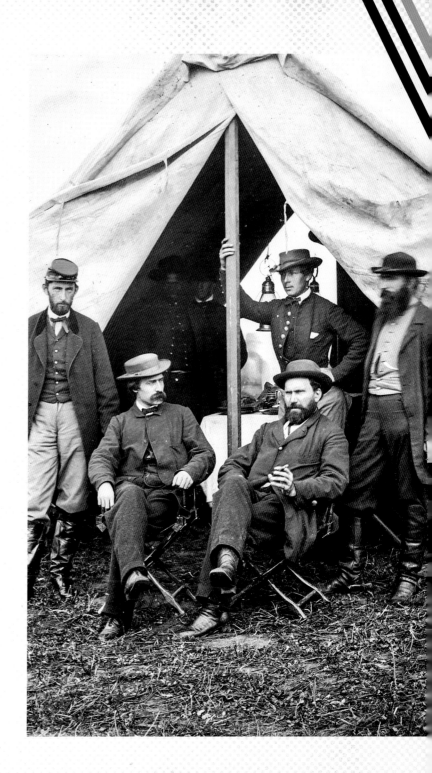

Allan Pinkerton, *seated on right*, talks with a group of his operatives in Antietam, Maryland, 1862.

BUILDING A SPY NETWORK

In response to Felton's concerns, Pinkerton came to Philadelphia in late January 1861 with a team of operatives. His work for PW&B would involve more than a simple investigation. To get the information he sought, Pinkerton's team would have to gain the trust of these Southern instigators, become part of their growing network, and spy on them.

Timothy Webster was one of Pinkerton's operatives. His assignment was to join a secret militia near Baltimore. He assumed the identity of a devoted and outspoken Southerner who hated the North. Webster took his convincing act to the small town of Perryman, Maryland, directly north of Baltimore. It did not take long for the likeable secret agent to gain the confidence of the townspeople, who then ushered him into their inner circle.

Meanwhile, Harry Davies, another Pinkerton agent, went to Baltimore and took on the role of a sophisticated Frenchman from New Orleans, Louisiana, who came east to support the secessionist movement. Other agents were involved, all playing the parts of Southern extremists.

In the weeks leading up to his March 4 inauguration, Lincoln planned to travel from his hometown of Springfield, Illinois, to Washington, DC, by train. A few friends accompanied the new president on the 13-day trip to the capital,

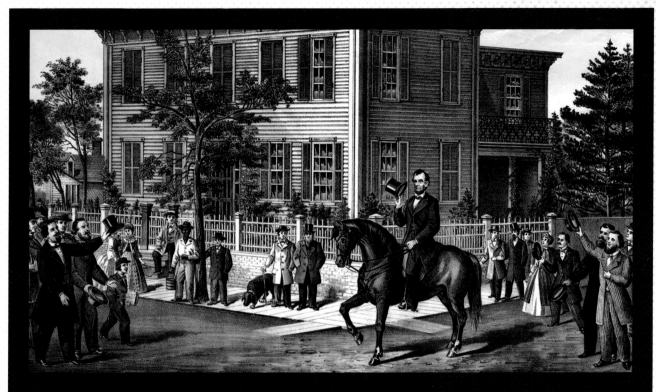

President-elect Abraham Lincoln greeted a crowd that had gathered in front of his home in Springfield, Illinois, in October 1860.

which began on February 11, 1861.[2] The president-elect made several stops along the way to greet supporters and speak about his plans for the nation's future.

THE ASSASSINATION PLOT

Only a few hours after Lincoln's train pulled out of Springfield, Davies, the Pinkerton undercover agent, was attending a meeting of secessionists at the

LINCOLN'S REACTION

In his memoir, *The Spy of the Rebellion*, Allan Pinkerton wrote about Abraham Lincoln's reaction when he first heard of the plot in Baltimore to take his life:

He had not evinced the slightest evidence of agitation or fear. Calm and self-possessed, his only sentiments seemed to be those of profound regret, that the Southern sympathizers could be so far led away by the excitement of the hour, as to consider his death a necessity for the furtherance of their cause.[3]

Barnum Hotel in Baltimore. At that meeting, Davies heard of a plot to stab Lincoln to death when the president-elect made a stop in Baltimore during the late-morning hours of February 23, 1861. The incoming president was scheduled to give a short address to a crowd of well-wishers from the platform at the Baltimore train station.

A few days after Davies got word of the plot to kill Lincoln, Webster was attending a meeting of the local militia he had joined in his undercover role in Perryman. There, he heard about the assassination plot in even greater detail. Both agents immediately informed their boss about what they had discovered.

Pinkerton began thinking of a plan to prevent the assassination. He sent an urgent message to Norman Judd, a close friend of Lincoln's and chairman of the Illinois Republican State Central Committee. Judd was making the journey to Washington, DC, with the president-elect. Pinkerton headed to Philadelphia to

UNWELCOME IN BALTIMORE

There has always been debate about whether Lincoln made the right decision by changing his plans based on the information gathered by Allan Pinkerton's spies. It turned out, however, that the plot to kill the new president was indeed real. The rest of Lincoln's party did cut through Baltimore on the way to Washington, DC, and stopped in the city at 11 a.m., as scheduled. The *Baltimore Sun*, a major daily newspaper, reported at the time that a jeering crowd was waiting for Lincoln to exit the train. When it became evident Lincoln was not on the train, the crowd spotted his luggage on a carriage to a hotel where Lincoln's friends and family were staying. The trunks were marked with a large "A. L." The crowd followed the luggage, heckling it the entire way as if it were the president-elect himself.

meet Lincoln's train, reveal his plan to protect the incoming president, and get him to the nation's capital safely.

On February 21, 1861, only a few days before the attempt on Lincoln's life was supposed to take place, Pinkerton met with the president-elect. He suggested Lincoln change his schedule. He also advised Lincoln to switch trains before heading through Baltimore, so his train would be going on a track different from the one the conspirators expected. Lincoln was reluctant to change any of his travel plans, even though Pinkerton assured the newly elected commander in chief the plot was real. The sixteenth president of the United States did not want to sneak into Washington, DC.

However, after speaking with Pinkerton, Lincoln received a message from General Winfield Scott, the commanding general of the US Army. Scott reported

the military had also heard about the assassination plot unfolding in Baltimore. Lincoln agreed to put the secret plan into action.

On February 22, Lincoln left Philadelphia for Harrisburg, the capital of Pennsylvania. After Lincoln attended a dinner meeting with supporters in Harrisburg, Pinkerton's force took him under the cover of darkness to a PW&B train yard not normally used for passenger transport. There, Lincoln got into a sleeper car outfitted to look like it was being used to transport a sick patient for medical care. It was connected to a train that would enter Baltimore at

Thanks to the efforts of Pinkerton and his team, Lincoln traveled through Baltimore unharmed, allowing him to deliver his inauguration speech on March 4, 1861.

3:30 a.m. on February 23, well ahead of Lincoln's scheduled 11:00 a.m. arrival. The car carrying Lincoln would have to connect to another train before heading into Washington, DC.[4]

Everything was going as planned until the connecting train was delayed. For two tense hours, Pinkerton and his force guarded the president-elect. Finally, at 5:30 a.m., the train arrived after normal delays. Lincoln reached Washington, DC, in time for a late breakfast. This was the first time a spy network had been used to track the activity of Southern sympathizers.

Later that day, Pinkerton arrived back in Baltimore and met with Davies. The undercover agent told Pinkerton the Lincoln conspirators had vowed revenge, not only on the new president, but on the spies in their midst who had betrayed them. For Pinkerton, those words meant there would be many more sleepless nights ahead.

SLEEPLESS IN HARRISBURG

The person who arranged for the sleeper car to carry Lincoln from Harrisburg to Baltimore was Kate Warne. A Pinkerton operative, Warne is believed to have been the first woman detective in the United States. She headed Pinkerton's Female Detective Bureau. She could handle a gun and helped guard the president-elect on his route. Lincoln was impressed by her work and thanked her in person. Lincoln told Warne, "I am sensible, ma'am of having put you to some inconvenience—not to speak of placing you in danger."[5]

Confederate troops launched a surprise attack on Union-held Fort Sumter near Charleston, South Carolina, on April 12, 1861, beginning the Civil War.

IN PLAIN SIGHT

The conspirators who plotted to kill Lincoln in Baltimore in February 1861 never discovered who had betrayed them. It would be decades before the names of Allan Pinkerton's operatives in that daring mission were revealed to the public.

But secessionists were still determined to rebel against Northern principles, especially the abolition of slavery. Southerners, who were passionate about states' rights, did not want the federal government passing laws interfering with their way of life, which depended on slavery.

The American Civil War (1861–1865) started in the early morning hours of April 12, 1861, when Confederate troops fired on Fort Sumter, a federal installation in Charleston Harbor, South Carolina. The attack on Fort Sumter came only 39 days after Lincoln took office as president of the United States. Lincoln's immediate reaction to the attack was to call for 75,000 militia volunteers from the loyal states.[1]

The seven states that had seceded from the Union had already voted to form the Confederate States of America, a separate nation from the United States. Following Lincoln's call for troops, four additional Southern states, Virginia, Arkansas, Tennessee, and North Carolina, seceded from the Union and joined the Confederacy. These states did not want to send troops to fight against their Southern neighbors. By June 8, the Confederacy had 11 states.

SPIES EVERYWHERE

Spying played a critical role in the Civil War. Yet, at the dawn of the conflict, neither the North nor the South had an organized military intelligence bureau or anything resembling a government-backed spying operation. What they did have were so-called citizen spies. These spies were willing to risk their lives for whichever side they supported.

Washington, DC, was a hub of undercover operatives. At the outset of the Civil War, the South had the upper hand on information gathering. Southerners distrusted Lincoln so much they had started sending citizen spies to the nation's capital as soon as he was elected president. In addition, many Southern sympathizers already lived in Washington, DC, and were eager to gather any information they could against Lincoln.

These secret operatives were firmly in place in Washington, DC, society by the time Lincoln took office on March 4, 1861. Their mission was to report any information circulating around the capital about what actions the new US president might take against the South. They were especially interested in his positions on slavery and the use of force to abolish it.

Some of the informants started spy rings, whereas others worked independently. They learned valuable information about the Northern military from contacts in the US government

Spies regularly attended public events, such as Lincoln's first inauguration on March 4, 1861, in Washington, DC.

who resigned their positions and swore allegiance to the Confederacy. Other informants chose to remain in their elected offices, where they had easy access to information. Spies focused on collecting solid facts about troop movements, geography and topography, military strategy, supply routes, equipment, morale among soldiers, and civilian support for the war.

The North drew on some key sources of information as well. Southerners who disagreed with secession gladly shared any information they had about the Confederate military with Northern commanders or elected officials they knew.

Richmond, Virginia, the Confederate capital, was only 100 miles (160 km) away from Washington, DC. The short distance between the two capitals made it relatively easy for citizen spies supporting the Union to travel to the Southern capital to gather information about Confederate war plans.

NEWSBOYS

Both the North and the South recruited boys as young as 12 years to be citizen spies. Disguised as newsboys, these youngsters went into military encampments, selling newspapers to troops. While they were there, they would talk to the soldiers and gather tactical information. Charles Phillips was only 14 years old when he got involved in espionage. He started out as a courier, simply relaying information that his father, John, a Union spy in Richmond, had given him. But after a short apprenticeship, Charles Phillips became an extremely capable spy himself, using the cover of a newsboy. Charles's role as a newsboy was fitting, as his father worked as a printer at the *Richmond Dispatch*.

By today's standards, spying during the Civil War was not difficult, though it was risky. In Washington, DC, for instance, people spoke freely and openly in stores, at parties, and on street corners about troop movements, military installations, and the latest innovations in weaponry. The nation had not yet recognized that neighbors might be spying on neighbors.

People suspected of spying for one side would be investigated by the military of the opposing side and, if evidence of spying was discovered, these individuals would be arrested and put on trial. If found guilty, they might go to prison or even be sentenced to death.

CITIZEN SPY RINGS

Only a few months after the attack on Fort Sumter, citizens and elected officials in the Northern states were demanding a quick and decisive victory over the Confederacy. Many Northerners believed this could be accomplished by capturing Richmond.

Despite his doubts about the readiness of his men, Union brigadier general Irvin McDowell, commander of the Union army of Northeastern Virginia, led his troops to Manassas Junction in Virginia, only 25 miles (40 km) from Washington, DC. The Union had learned Confederate troops had taken up positions near Bull Run Creek in Manassas.

McDowell's objective was to crush the Confederate army gathered at Bull Run and then move on to Richmond. He planned to accomplish this by launching a surprise attack on the rebel troops. But the South was ready to meet McDowell's forces.

The First Battle of Bull Run, fought on July 21, 1861, ended up being the bloodiest battle in US history up to that point. Both sides sustained heavy losses, with Union troops retreating and Confederate troops holding their ground. Not only had the Southern army repulsed the Northern attack, they sent Union troops running back to Washington, DC, in turmoil. It was as if the Southern army, under the leadership of General P. G. T. Beauregard, knew in advance about the Union plans for attack. In fact, Beauregard did know about the surprise attack, and the information came from a highly unlikely source.

A SUCCESSFUL SOUTHERN SPY RING

In late 1860, Union army captain Thomas Jordan began setting up a Confederate spy ring. Jordan was born in Virginia and secretly remained a Southern sympathizer until he resigned from the Union army in May 1861 and joined the Confederate army.

The spy ring Jordan set up was especially helpful during the early months of secession. Because of his position in the Union army, Jordan was able to convey a great deal of information to the fledgling Confederacy, including reports that the Northern army did not plan to take any immediate military action against the secessionists. In his painstaking efforts to put together a strong spy ring, Jordan approached Rose O'Neal Greenhow.

Greenhow was raised along the Maryland shore. She moved to Washington, DC, in 1828 as a teenager and began working her way into the capital city's high society. By the time the Civil War broke out, Greenhow had many influential friends in the Union who held high political appointments and powerful government jobs. Only those closest to her, however, knew of her Southern leanings.

Jordan learned about Greenhow from Virginia governor John Letcher,

Before the Civil War, Thomas Jordan attended the US Military Academy at West Point and served with the US Army.

ETERNAL GRATITUDE

The Confederate government and military leaders never forgot how much Rose O'Neal Greenhow's espionage effort meant in their victory at the First Battle of Bull Run. After the battle, Greenhow received a message from Thomas Jordan, who was serving as the Confederate army's adjutant general, the officer with the authority to speak and write for the commander. "Our President and our General direct me to thank you. We rely upon you for further information. The Confederacy owes you a debt," the note read.[3]

who was a longtime friend of hers. When Jordan asked Greenhow to join his spy ring in early 1861, she happily agreed. "I am a Southern woman born with revolutionary blood in my veins," she said.[2] By April, Greenhow had become the ring's spymaster, or leader.

Greenhow's spy ring was elaborate, with many operatives and a sophisticated method of transporting messages to Southern commanders. For example, Greenhow worked with some female couriers who sewed messages in their skirts or who hid notes in their long thick hair. Early in the war, few suspected Greenhow of espionage.

Through her Union contacts, Greenhow provided General Beauregard with detailed information about the North's secret plans to attack Confederate troops at Bull Run Creek. Greenhow knew about anticipated Union troop movements and how many troops there were. She even obtained copies of maps used by the Union to formulate the attack.

Because of the information Greenhow gave him, Beauregard not only was prepared for the Union onslaught, but had reinforcements there to back him up. Reserve troops had been in the Shenandoah Valley in Virginia, and could never have gotten to Manassas in time if Beauregard had not been warned in advance about McDowell's plan.

Greenhow lived on Sixteenth Street Northwest in Washington, DC, and General Beauregard was always fond of saying he never doubted the information he got from a woman "who lived within easy rifle range of the White House."[4] The spy operation Greenhow ran became one of the most notorious spy rings of the war. "I employed every capacity with which God has endowed me," Greenhow later wrote, "and the result was far more successful than my hopes could have flattered me to expect."[5]

Rose O'Neal Greenhow, shown here with her daughter, remained in Washington, DC, for the first year of the war.

THE PERFECT SPY

Spying is not for the fainthearted. Besides being brave, spies have to be smart, observant, handy, imaginative, clever, and quick on their feet. They may speak multiple languages and master a variety of dialects and accents. Spies assume numerous identities. They must have a good memory because they rarely have the opportunity to write down all the material they collect.

Spies tend to be good actors, picking up on the mannerisms, slang and local expressions, behavior, likes, and dislikes of the people they are around. That way they can fit in and build trust.

A good spy is tight-lipped, knowing how to gather key information while not giving out too much information of his or her own. Developing a trusted network of sources is vital to any spy, as is knowing who has valuable information and who does not.

In the Civil War, spies had to be daring and adventurous. They often stayed out in the field for a long time under harsh conditions, gathering the intelligence they needed to change the course of a battle or even the entire war.

Secret service operatives pose for a photo at Pinkerton's headquarters in October 1862.

General George B. McClellan arrives to take control of the Union army.

SPYING BY THE MILITARY

After the Union defeat at the First Battle of Bull Run on July 21, 1861, President Lincoln put General George B. McClellan in charge of the defense of the US capital and named him commander of the Army of the Potomac. The general had been victorious in several skirmishes early in the Civil War.

McClellan offered Pinkerton the job of rooting out Southern spies who had taken up residence in Washington, DC. Pinkerton was excited to work with McClellan again. The two had worked together when McClellan was chief engineer and later vice president of the Illinois Central Railroad between 1857 and 1858. The men became close friends.

FOCUS ON COUNTERESPIONAGE

Many Union leaders believed their plans for the First Battle of Bull Run had been leaked to the enemy. So one of McClellan's first actions as commander of the Army of the Potomac was to order Pinkerton to set up a counterespionage unit and an intelligence-gathering force.

In response to that order, Pinkerton established the secret service of the Army of the Potomac, one of the first military intelligence units of the war. He brought in many of the undercover agents he had employed in the past, including Timothy Webster. Pinkerton worked under the assumed identity of Major E. J. Allen.

MILITARY INFORMATION MANAGEMENT

Brigadier General James Garfield was the chief of staff for Major General William S. Rosecrans, commander of the Union Army of the Cumberland in Tennessee. While in this job in 1863, Garfield created one of the most efficient intelligence units in the Union army. Garfield used data from a variety of sources, including spies. Garfield's approach differed from that of earlier spy networks. He organized all the information he obtained and analyzed how it affected all the military operations throughout the region covered by the Union Army of the Cumberland. Before that, each piece of information had been acted on individually with no regard for how it related to the overall war effort. Garfield's comprehensive approach made for more effective military operations. Garfield was widely recognized for his work in army intelligence. After the war, he went into politics. In 1880, Garfield was elected the twentieth president of the United States.

Pinkerton approached his job from several angles. He searched for domestic moles—people living in the North who were spies for the South. He also sent agents of his own behind enemy lines to gather information about the Confederacy. In addition, Pinkerton's operatives watched enemy troop movements and reported where Confederate camps were being set up.

TARGETING ROSE O'NEAL GREENHOW

In his undercover work in Washington, DC, Pinkerton kept hearing one name time and again: Rose O'Neal Greenhow. Greenhow's easy access to many prominent Union officials and military men, as well as her Southern leanings, made him suspicious of her. Then came word from Webster, who was working undercover in Baltimore as a rebellious Southern activist, that many Confederate soldiers considered Greenhow their secret weapon up North.

By August 23, 1861, Pinkerton believed he had enough evidence on Greenhow. He put her under house arrest and then sent her to prison for the next nine months.[1] In June 1862, Greenhow was allowed to leave Washington, DC, for Richmond under an agreement that she would not return North until after the war. Pinkerton viewed the capture of Greenhow as one of his greatest cases.

However, there were times that Pinkerton's intelligence gathering was faulty. He and his agents often overestimated Confederate troop strength, basing it on

President Lincoln consults with Allan Pinkerton, *left*, and Major General John A. McClernand in Antietam, Maryland, in 1862.

the number of rations rather than the count of soldiers who actually went into battle. That led McClellan to believe his army was outnumbered by Confederate troops on several occasions. As a result, the general sometimes hesitated to attack, missing opportunities to crush the Confederate army. In the spring of 1862, for example, McClellan delayed his Peninsula Campaign for more than a month because of troop miscalculations and bad intelligence. The campaign was designed to capture the Confederate capital of Richmond.

Pinkerton thought the Confederates had 150,000 soldiers poised to repel McClellan's 120,000-man offensive, so the general waited for reinforcements before attacking. Actually, Confederate forces numbered only 50,000.[2] The delay gave Southern troops time to fortify their positions and get reinforcements of their own. The Confederates held off the Union army and McClellan never made it to Richmond.

Following the Battle of Antietam in September 1862, Lincoln was beginning to lose patience with McClellan. The president traveled to McClellan's headquarters in Antietam to meet with the general and Pinkerton. Lincoln urged McClellan to attack Confederate troops as they retreated, but the general refused.

ROSE O'NEAL GREENHOW

1814–1864

Maria Rosetta "Rose" O'Neale was born in 1814 in Montgomery County, Maryland. The family dropped the e from the end of their last name when Rose was a child. Rose's father died when she was only three years old, and her widowed mother struggled to raise five daughters. Overwhelmed by the task, she sent Rose to live with her aunt in the nation's capital.

By the time Rose moved to Washington, DC, she was a striking young woman. She dated many eligible bachelors in powerful jobs in government but married Dr. Robert Greenhow of Virginia. Dr. Greenhow worked for the State Department. Through her husband, Rose met all the country's leading politicians.

Dr. Greenhow died in 1857 and Rose was once again courted by the rich and famous of Washington, DC, but she never remarried. Her contacts in the federal government made her the perfect Confederate spy. Her spying activities on behalf of the South earned her the nickname Rebel Rose.

Exiled to Richmond in the spring of 1862, she was hailed by Southerners as a heroine. She traveled through Europe from 1863 to 1864, drumming up support for the Southern cause. While returning to the United States in October 1864, her ship ran aground in rough waters off the North Carolina coast. Greenhow tried to get ashore in a rowboat, but waves capsized the rowboat and she drowned.

OTHER LEADERS HIRE THEIR OWN SPIES

Nevertheless, McClellan started a trend when he asked Pinkerton to set up an intelligence unit for the Army of the Potomac. Other Union generals quickly followed suit. In early 1862, General Winfield Scott, the commanding general of the Union army, hired Lafayette Baker to be his chief of intelligence. Baker was a member of the famous vigilance committee of San Francisco, California, which worked to rid that city of crime and corruption. In reality, however, Baker had limited hands-on experience in conducting investigations and spying.

When the Civil War broke out, Baker, a native New Yorker, went back East. He arranged a meeting with Scott and convinced the aging general he was meant to be a spy and could handle the commander's intelligence operation. Flamboyant, brash, and persistent, Baker got Scott's attention and the job. Baker set up what he called a secret service unit for Scott. From then on, Baker and Pinkerton clashed. They refused to coordinate their efforts, and on several occasions the two men inadvertently arrested each other's operatives.

President Lincoln had his own intelligence operative who reported directly to him. William Lloyd had the perfect cover. Lloyd, who published travel guides, always had a reason to be traveling through the South to gather information for his publications. Lincoln paid him to report on Confederate fortifications, as well as troop movements and troop strength. Lloyd also told Lincoln about any activities he witnessed involving Union troops, giving the president a way to check on his own commanders. Lloyd's work was extremely secretive. Not even Lincoln's closest advisers knew the president had hired Lloyd in July 1861 and kept him on the job throughout the war.

By late 1862, Lincoln had grown tired of McClellan's timid and overcautious military strategy, and he replaced him with General Ambrose Burnside as head of the Army of the Potomac. In protest, Pinkerton resigned from his post as the Army of the Potomac's secret service chief. Burnside served as McClellan's replacement for only a few months. On January 26, 1863, Major General Joseph Hooker was assigned to take his place. Hooker ordered Colonel George H. Sharpe to take over Pinkerton's role.

Sharpe, who was eventually promoted to the rank of general, established the Bureau of Military Information. Under Sharpe's leadership the bureau became one of the best-organized and most professional spy operations in the war for either side. Sharpe understood the importance of compiling accurate information, making sure his informants were reliable, and confirming the information he got through various other sources.

SIGNAL CORPS

Both the Union and the Confederate armies had signal corps. The corps played a key role for each side. Trained members of the corps used signal flags to pass along orders, send warnings, and inform commanders about victories and defeats on different fronts of the battlefield. Members of the signal corps were also involved with other forms of communication, such as telegraphs, and worked to intercept messages sent by the enemy.

The Confederate Signal Corps, founded in 1862, was run by the Confederate War Department. Unlike the Union Signal Corps, it had an espionage component, called the Secret Service Bureau. Besides being in charge of spying missions against the North, the bureau also conducted counterespionage operations. This was done to unearth Northern spies operating in Southern territory.

One of the crucial tasks of the Confederate Secret Service Bureau was making sure vital information collected by Confederate spies working undercover deep inside enemy territory reached officials in

SAFE HOUSES

Both sides in the Civil War had safe houses. These were homes of sympathizers, often located inside enemy territory, where spies could go if they needed help. Sometimes spies would take shelter in a safe house just to hide. But they would also seek out a safe house if they were wounded and needed medical attention. At times, spies used safe houses to hide sensitive documents, such as maps showing where enemy encampments were located or drawings of fortifications. It was not safe to transport such documents to a military headquarters, even in friendly territory. Safe houses had many hiding places where both people and objects could be concealed if enemy troops came to search the house. Those hiding places included compartments hidden under the floor, cupboards, closets, attic crawl spaces, and secret rooms.

From the top of Lookout Mountain in Chattanooga, Tennessee, the Union army signal corps sent messages to the Union encampments below.

Richmond. To do this, the bureau set up a so-called Secret Line. This line was made up of couriers, usually riding on horseback but at times traveling by horse-drawn wagon. They followed special trails, along which safe houses were located, to get messages from Southern spies in the North to Confederate government and military leaders. The Secret Service Bureau proved to be one of the South's most effective military spy networks.

DOCTORS' LINE

Besides setting up the Secret Line, the Confederate Secret Service Bureau came up with the ingenious idea of the Doctors' Line. During the Civil War, it was customary for doctors to make house calls. They went out at all hours, carrying large medical bags, without arousing any suspicion. Doctors who were Southern sympathizers would transport messages from spies in their medical bags, dropping those messages at the houses of couriers, who would then take them to Confederate generals.

Spies lived under the constant threat of being discovered and shot.

RFA-SHAR

SPY RINGS

Despite the successes of the South's Secret Service Bureau, some Confederate commanders established their own teams of spies. They wanted operatives they had trained, knew well, and trusted completely. Among those generals was James Ewell Brown "Jeb" Stuart.

Stuart was one of the South's greatest cavalrymen, excelling in reconnaissance and intelligence gathering. Although Stuart gathered a great deal of valuable intelligence, he was not a spy himself. He had skilled spies working for him, and he relied on two spy rings operating out of Washington, DC, to keep him informed of the Union's every move. One of those rings was coordinated by Captain Thomas Nelson Conrad.

STUART'S SPIES

Conrad joined the Third Virginia Cavalry early in the war and was made a chaplain. He was not ordained but was a well-known lay Methodist preacher. While he fulfilled his duties as a spiritual adviser, he also undertook daring spy missions in Washington, DC.

Before the war, Conrad had been the headmaster at the Georgetown Institute, a boys' preparatory school in Washington, DC. There was no neighborhood more pro-Confederacy in Washington, DC, than Georgetown. Conrad had many friends in Georgetown and he knew all the Southern sympathizers. It was easy for him to assemble an eager and willing ring of informants.

One of those people was a clerk in the Union War Department. On at least one occasion, the clerk purposely left reports and maps on his desk when he went out to lunch so Conrad could sneak in, review the documents, and send the information to Stuart. That data included precise information on Northern positions for the Union's proposed attack on Richmond during General George McClellan's Peninsula Campaign in the spring of 1862.

Conrad was bold and cagey. It took the Union nearly half the war to catch on to the work he was doing to undermine the Union. Even in mid-1863, when Lafayette Baker and his Union counterespionage squad learned of Conrad's activities, the Southern spy managed to elude them. One of Baker's own agents,

Edward Norton, was a member of Conrad's spy ring and tipped the enterprising spy that Baker's operatives were on their way to arrest him. Conrad slipped out of Washington, DC, and went to Richmond. Even after that close call, Conrad kept venturing into the federal capital and gathering vital intelligence for the South until the war ended.

Benjamin Franklin "Frank" Stringfellow, 21 years old at the start of the Civil War, was another of Stuart's operatives. Stringfellow's first mission was to put together a spy ring in Alexandria, Virginia, in late 1861. To accomplish his goal, Stringfellow posed as a dental assistant and apprentice, even though he had no dental training whatsoever. The dentist he worked with, Dr. Richard Sykes, was a Southern sympathizer and let Stringfellow live in his home.

BREAKING NEWS

The details published in articles in Northern newspapers about Union military strategy during the Civil War were often so exact that spies simply sent the information to Confederate commanders. For example, before the Battle of Chickamauga in southeastern Tennessee and northwestern Georgia on September 19–20, 1863, a spy gave Confederate general Braxton Bragg an article from the *New York Times* that explained how the Union was going to try to get Bragg to shift his position during the battle. So the general stayed put. That information helped prevent Union troops from seizing territory in Georgia during the battle.

Stringfellow's mission was to write daily reports on Union troop movements and firepower. Some of the information he gathered came from Southern citizen spies. Additional details on Northern troop activities came from events that he witnessed himself, and he also picked up information from Northern newspapers. Newspapers in both the North and South often carried detailed stories about Union or Confederate strategies for the war, written by reporters who were at the front. Southern military leaders used these readily available materials to help plan counteroffensives against Northern troops. Northern generals found stories about Confederate troop movements and troop strength in Southern newspapers as well. Union general Ulysses S. Grant was an avid reader of Southern newspapers whenever he could get them.

Confederate spies also placed coded personal ads in newspapers to send messages to government officials in Richmond. The Confederate Secret Service Bureau often had couriers and spies collect these newspapers. But getting them into Southern hands was tricky because the newspapers were bulky and hard to transport.

Stringfellow would read the newspapers, summarize the information contained in them, and send a report to Stuart on only a few sheets of paper every day. He carried out this assignment until late February 1862, when Union soldiers learned of his espionage activity. As they came to arrest him one night, Stringfellow made a bold escape. He wandered the countryside avoiding federal troops until early spring, when he rejoined Stuart near Yorktown, Virginia.

Stringfellow went on many more undercover operations throughout the war. His missions took him deep behind enemy lines, where he traveled by night in

Newspapers in both the North and the South became key sources for information about war strategy during the Civil War.

disguise. He always carried papers identifying himself as a dentist. He would present them to Union patrols if they stopped and questioned him. Information supplied by Stringfellow helped the Confederacy win battles at Cedar Mountain and Groveton in Virginia, as well as the Second Battle of Bull Run on August 30, 1862. Stringfellow often worked with other noted Confederate scouts and spies, including the legendary Colonel John Mosby. Though Mosby was better known for his efforts as a guerrilla fighter than as a scout or a spy, he worked with Stringfellow on several key missions.

VAN LEW'S OPERATIVES

The Union had its own spy rings, one of which was located right in the Confederate capital city of Richmond. Elizabeth Van Lew was among Virginia's most prominent citizens, but she was a Northern sympathizer. The daughter of wealthy Virginians, Van Lew was born in 1818. She had Northern roots. Her father, John, was from Long Island, New York, and her mother, Eliza, hailed from Philadelphia. Both moved to Virginia in the early 1800s. John moved for health reasons, whereas Eliza came to live with her older brother after her parents died.

In the early 1830s, Van Lew was sent to a Quaker school in Philadelphia, where her parents believed the schooling was better than in the South. There the young woman acquired her abolitionist views. She called slavery "arrogant . . . intrusive . . . and cruel."[1] After the attack on Fort Sumter, Van Lew made a commitment to help the Union abolish slavery. "Never did a feeling of more calm determination and high resolve for endurance come over me," she said of her work to bring an end to slavery.[2]

Richmond had a core of Union supporters among its citizenry. Van Lew set out to organize them and use information they gathered from Confederate soldiers and elected officials who unwittingly gave out information to people they thought supported the Southern cause.

Van Lew never married and was considered odd. She used that image to her benefit as a cover for her spy activities during the war. She walked around muttering to herself with her hair uncombed and her clothes old and ragged. She earned the nickname of "Crazy Bet" and most Confederate troops thought she was harmless.[3]

The image she cultivated allowed her to visit Union prisoners of war at Libby Prison in Richmond. Her visits began soon after the First Battle of Bull Run, as the first captured Union soldiers began to arrive there. In the prison she gathered intelligence from Union prisoners. These prisoners learned about Confederate

Union spy Elizabeth Van Lew

troop movements when they overheard their guards talking about the latest news from the front.

Van Lew also had a room in her large home with a bookcase that rotated and then locked in place. Behind the bookcase was a secret room, where prisoners who escaped from Libby Prison could hide until it was safe for them to leave Richmond.

At one point in the war, the Confederate army confiscated all horses from the residents of Richmond to use in the war. Van Lew hid one of her horses in that secret room in case she needed to go on horseback to deliver a message to the Union high command herself. As the war went on, Van Lew's spy network expanded and her spy ring rivaled any other in size and effectiveness.

DIEHARD ABOLITIONIST

John and Eliza, the parents of Elizabeth Van Lew, owned a mansion in Richmond and had slaves. After her father's death in 1843, Van Lew, then 25 years old, freed all the family's slaves and offered to hire any of them who wanted to stay on as servants. She paid them well and built up close friendships with them. Even before she was able to free them, Van Lew was friendly with the slaves and taught many of them to read and write. Van Lew was so opposed to slavery that she used her inheritance to buy slaves who were related to the slaves she had freed, and she freed those people as well. She was roundly criticized in her hometown of Richmond for her actions.

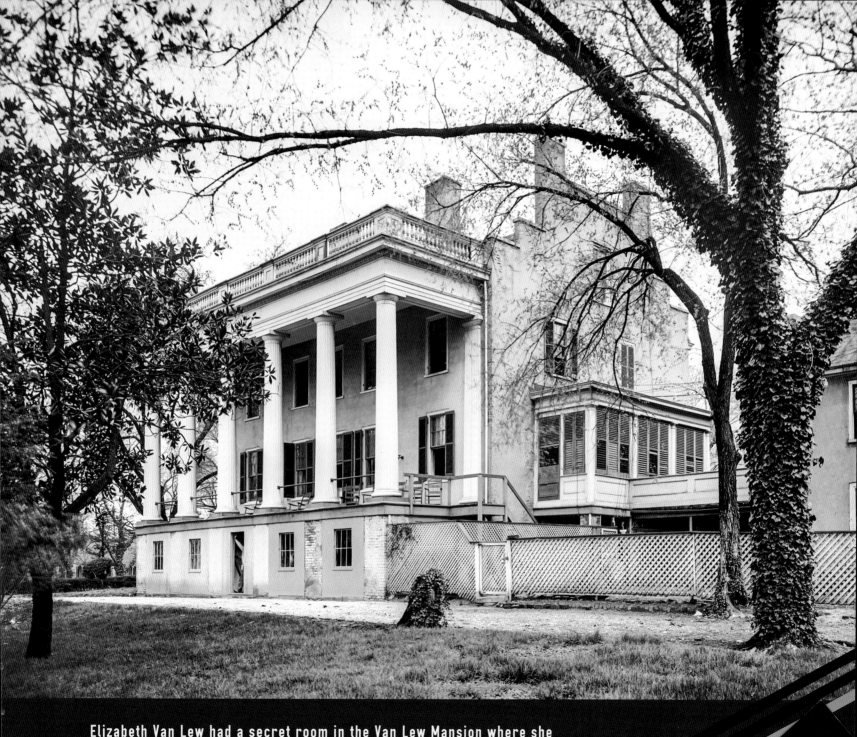

Elizabeth Van Lew had a secret room in the Van Lew Mansion where she sometimes hid Northern officers who had escaped from prisoner of war camps.

COURIERS
A SPYMASTER'S SECRET WEAPON

Spymasters such as Rose O'Neal Greenhow and Elizabeth Van Lew had very effective networks of couriers. These couriers risked their lives carrying coded messages through enemy lines to generals and other military personnel in the field. Couriers would be treated as spies if they were caught. Van Lew established five relay stations between Richmond and the Union front lines. Each relay station had rested couriers and fresh horses. Each courier at the relay station took a message from the incoming courier and left with it immediately on the next leg of the journey.

Couriers had to be able to move swiftly, think quickly, and, if they were stopped by enemy troops, have a reasonable explanation as to why they were passing through that territory. For instance, on one occasion Van Lew drained the contents out of some eggs and placed coded messages written on thin paper inside the eggshells. Van Lew also concealed messages in baskets with false bottoms and put food over the false bottoms. The courier could then say he was bringing food to the front.

One courier for the Confederates was known to travel back and forth from Washington, DC, to Maryland with a wagon filled with horse manure. Messages from Confederate spies were hidden under the manure.

African-American spies, including some believed to have worked in the homes of Confederate leaders, proved to be very effective at spying for the North.

BLACK DISPATCHES

Throughout the Civil War, slaves and runaway slaves were among the most crucial sources of information for the Union army. Some slaves agreed to give up their own freedom and remain in bondage to gather valuable intelligence for the North. Some free African Americans who lived in the North risked their freedom and their very lives by leaving the safety of the Union and working undercover as spies in the South. The reports made by these brave African Americans were classified by the Union military as "black dispatches."

PLANTING SPIES

Van Lew was one of the Union spymasters who came up with the idea of planting African Americans as servants in the homes of influential Southerners to spy on them. Van Lew and other Union spymasters realized that Southerners considered African Americans menial, uneducated servants, and simply ignored them. That gave these spies a perfect cover.

One of Van Lew's best African-American agents was believed to be a woman named Mary Elizabeth Bowser. Bowser, who was extremely well educated, had attended a Quaker school for African Americans in Philadelphia. She was said to have a photographic memory and could recall documents she had read word for word.

Van Lew heard that Confederate president Jefferson Davis and his family were looking for servants they could trust to tend to their needs in the Confederate White House in Richmond. Working behind the scenes, Van Lew is believed to have managed to place Bowser as one of the servants in the Davis household.

Bowser is believed to have taken on the name of Ellen Bond and pretended to be illiterate. She worked at the Confederate White House from early 1863 to the end of the Civil War in 1865. Confederate president Davis, his wife Varina, and

HIGH PRAISE

Many Northern leaders gave credit to black dispatches during the Civil War, including Union secretary of war Edwin M. Stanton and Colonel (later General) George H. Sharpe on the Virginia front and General Grenville Dodge on the western front. However, the greatest compliment came from Confederate general-in-chief Robert E. Lee, who was aware of all the information African Americans were passing along to Union forces during the war. He said the black dispatches were without a doubt "the chief source of information to the enemy."[1]

many Confederate government leaders and generals who came to the Confederate White House talked openly in front of Bowser. She then got the information she overheard to Van Lew. On some days Bowser was in the room serving food and clearing dishes when Davis met with his cabinet and Confederate general Robert E. Lee. Davis left top-secret documents around the house and on his desk, never suspecting his servant could not only read them, but remember them in their entirety.

Bowser often gave cryptic messages to Thomas McNiven to deliver to Van Lew. McNiven was a well-known baker in Richmond. No one in the Confederate capital realized McNiven worked for years as a Union spy. He delivered baked goods every day to the Confederate White House. When Bowser spoke with McNiven as he unloaded his wagon at the presidential mansion, no one suspected the two might be exchanging sensitive information.

Bowser was not the only undercover African-American agent to infiltrate the Confederate White House. William A.

COMMITTED TO MEMORY

Many African Americans who worked as spies for the North in the Civil War had razor-sharp memories. They gathered precise information about the number of Confederate troops they saw, the direction in which they were heading, the type of weapons they were carrying, and how quickly the troops were moving. The spies remembered the details without taking written notes, leaving no evidence that they were collecting information for the North if they happened to be stopped by Confederate troops. Had the spies been caught with that kind of evidence, Southern troops or Southern sympathizers would have killed the spies immediately. Northern scouts and officers were often amazed by the detail and accuracy of the information provided by black dispatches.

Jackson was the Confederate president's coachman. He drove Davis around Richmond in a horse-drawn carriage. Davis often discussed the progress of the war with high-ranking government and military officials while riding in the carriage with Jackson at the reins.

Jackson is believed to have deliberately listened in on those conversations and reported the details to Northern military leaders on the front lines in Virginia. He often left the presidential compound at night, crossed the front lines, and returned before anyone knew he was gone. Jackson overheard that the Confederates were having trouble getting supplies. He told Union military leaders

William A. Jackson not only drove Confederate president Jefferson Davis to all of his appointments, he also reported all he heard the president say to Union spies.

THE WRIGHT MOVES

In June 1863, African-American slave Charlie Wright fled from bondage on a plantation in Culpepper, Virginia. When he reached Union lines, Wright shared valuable information about the Confederate troop movements of General Robert E. Lee. The Union army had not been able to determine in which direction Lee and his troops were heading or if they had stopped their forward advance and set up camp in Culpepper. Wright, however, saw that Lee's forces were on the move northward. His report would prove to be one of the most important black dispatches of the war.

Based on Wright's observations, Union troops, led by General Joseph Hooker, shadowed Lee's forces and realized that he was going to Pennsylvania. As a result of Wright's detailed surveillance, the Union army took up key positions in south-central Pennsylvania in preparation for the critical Battle of Gettysburg, on July 1–3, 1863. The Union victory at Gettysburg was a turning point in the Civil War.

how they could use the Confederate supply shortages to their advantage. Late in the war, Davis knew there was an intelligence leak coming from his White House, but he never suspected Bowser or Jackson of being involved. To this day there are those who believe the stories of their espionage have been made up or exaggerated.

DISCOVERING SHIPBUILDING SECRETS

Mary Louvestre was an enslaved housekeeper for a Confederate ship engineer in Norfolk, Virginia. In July 1861, she overheard her master speaking with another ship designer and a Confederate naval officer. They were discussing the development of a new type of ship made of iron, rather than wood. This new ship would be built from the hull of the USS *Merrimack*, an old Union navy frigate that had been sunk in the Norfolk Navy Yard right after the Civil War began in April 1861.

The three men Louvestre overheard were convinced this newly outfitted ironclad ship would tip the war in the South's favor. They believed the wooden Union ships patrolling the Southern coast would be no match for the ironclad and would be easily sunk. Those Union ships were blockading Southern ports, making it difficult for the South to get weapons and supplies to Confederate troops.

Louvestre, who happened to be a talented artist, found the plans for the ironclad in her master's desk and traced them. Her drawings were exact replicas of the actual plans. At that time, the Union navy was trying to get funding to build its own ironclad ship, called the USS *Monitor*. But the US Congress was not convinced an ironclad was needed and was holding up the funding.

By the winter of 1862, Louvestre convinced her master to allow her to visit a former master of hers, who was ailing. But she was actually planning to travel to Washington, DC, with the plans and other information she had gathered about the *Merrimack*. She delivered the plans to US navy secretary Gideon Welles. Due to Louvestre's efforts, Congress gave the US Navy the funds it needed to build the USS *Monitor*.

In the naval battle at Hampton Roads, Virginia, the Union's *Monitor*, *left*, was able to save the Northern fleet from the Southern attack.

On March 9, 1862, the *Monitor* battled the *Merrimack*, which the South had renamed the CSS *Virginia*. The two ships battered each other with heavy firepower in Hampton Roads, a harbor at the mouth of the James River in Virginia. The naval battle went on for four hours and ended in a draw. However, the *Monitor* saved the US Navy from being destroyed by the Confederate ironclad. Without Louvestre's information, the North would have been defenseless against the CSS *Virginia*.

ON LINE

Dabney, known by just one name, and his wife were African-American slaves in Fredericksburg, Virginia. They escaped in 1863 and crossed Union army lines when the Northern army was camped along the banks of the Rappahannock River. Dabney became a paid cook for the Union army. He was fascinated by how the army used signal flags to communicate with troops off in the distance. So the soldiers taught Dabney about the signal system.

Shortly after the couple arrived at the Union camp, Mrs. Dabney asked the Union army for permission to return to Fredericksburg. Her request was granted. In Fredericksburg she became a servant once again, this time in the headquarters of a Confederate general. The headquarters was in full view of the Union encampment. Not long after his wife left, Dabney began giving the Union reports about Confederate troop movements. His information was always accurate and up-to-the-minute. Because Dabney never left camp, Union officers wondered how he came by this information.

As it turned out, Dabney and his wife had worked out a signal system before she left, based on the one he learned from the Union soldiers. Mrs. Dabney would hang laundry on the clothesline in a particular order that would let her husband know when Confederate troops were moving out. When he was asked how he gathered this intelligence, Dabney explained the couple's signal system to a Union officer. Pointing to the clothesline, he said, "That . . . gray shirt is [Confederate General James] Longstreet; and when she takes it off [the line], it means he's gone down to Richmond. That white shirt means [General Ambrose Powell] Hill; and when she moves it up to the west end of the line, Hill's corps has moved upstream."[2] Union General Joseph Hooker supposedly claimed the intelligence he received from Dabney was the most reliable and timely of the war.

LOST TO HISTORY

To protect the identity of spies or just due to poor record keeping, details of the work of many Civil War espionage agents, including a number of African Americans, were lost, destroyed, or never committed to writing. Yet, the black dispatches were considered vital to the Northern victory. Many runaway slaves willingly gave crucial intelligence to Northern forces with hope that the Union army would win the war, the nation would be reunited, and slavery would be abolished throughout the United States.

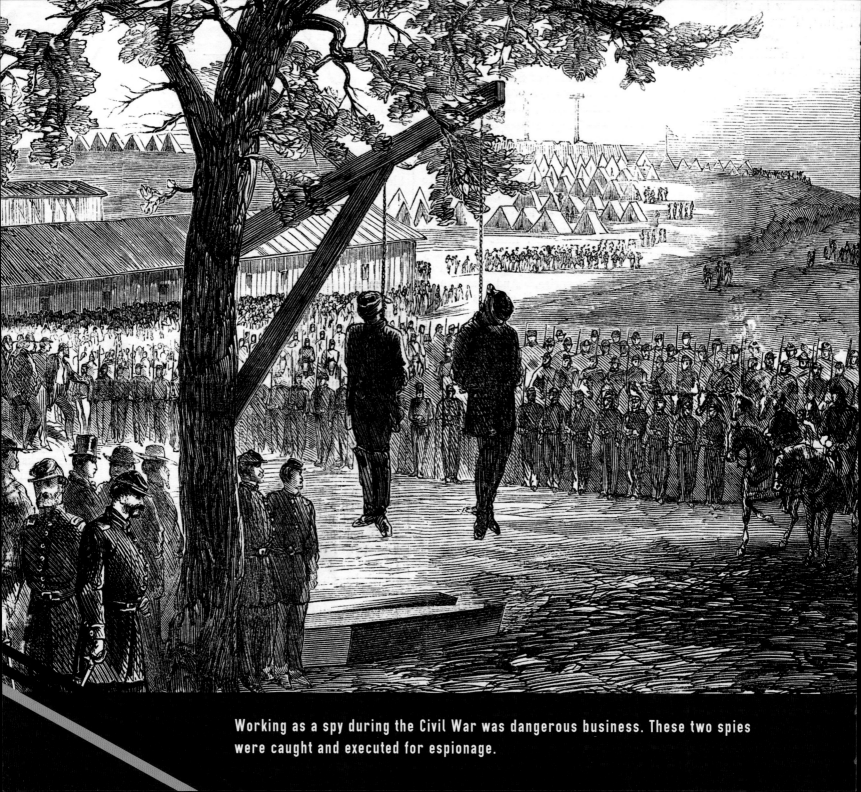

Working as a spy during the Civil War was dangerous business. These two spies were caught and executed for espionage.

DOUBLE AGENTS

Double agents are the most daring of all spies and undercover operatives working in the field of espionage. They pretend to be working as a spy for one intelligence-gathering agency or government, but in reality are loyal to another one, the enemy. Double agents have to remain extremely cool under pressure. A blown cover usually means death for a double agent.

Because of the dangerous nature of this work, few stories about double agents ever surface. These operatives' real identities are forever safeguarded and details of their missions kept secret. However, the exploits of a few double agents during the Civil War have come to light and illustrate the important role these fearless spies played in the conflict.

Allan Pinkerton, *left*, talks with secret servicemen in Cumberland Landing, Virginia, in 1862.

TIMOTHY WEBSTER: THE NORTH'S MOST DANGEROUS SPY

After helping to foil the assassination plot against Lincoln in February 1861, Timothy Webster continued working with Allan Pinkerton. When Pinkerton became General McClellan's intelligence chief in the summer of 1861, he brought Webster, then 40 years old, along with him as one of his spies.

Webster had already developed a reputation as a fearless Southern sympathizer. He did this while working undercover for Pinkerton in Baltimore during the Lincoln case. Webster continued in that role, traveling between Maryland and Virginia in 1861 and 1862. The spy was so convincing that he was practically considered a hero in lofty Confederate circles. All the while, Webster was reporting everything he heard or saw in the South to Pinkerton.

The spy's main objective was to get as close to the Confederate leadership, including Confederate president Davis, as he could. To help Webster accomplish his goal, Pinkerton came up with an ingenious plan.

In the course of his investigation of the Confederate spy Rose Greenhow in Washington, DC, Pinkerton had found a secret Confederate codebook. The codebook contained the secret cipher Greenhow used to communicate with Southern generals. The Confederates did not know Pinkerton had found the book. Another Pinkerton agent, Kate Warne, who had also worked on the Lincoln case, labored tirelessly to duplicate Greenhow's flowery handwriting. Once Warne mastered the handwriting, Pinkerton had her write messages to Greenhow's Southern contacts, such as General Beauregard. The messages, in Greenhow's handwriting and written in Confederate code, contained bogus information about Northern war plans. The man carrying the messages to the Confederates was Webster.

Pinkerton at a Union camp during the Civil War

He began delivering the messages in September 1861. The Pinkerton plan was designed to confuse the Southern military while elevating Webster's status among his Southern compatriots. The plan worked on both counts, and Webster became more revered by the Confederates than ever. He was even inducted into the Knights of Liberty, a radical and violent secret society of Southern sympathizers bent on overthrowing the federal government.

Webster's membership in the Knights of Liberty proved fruitful. On November 28, 1861, Thanksgiving Day, the society held a secret meeting to finalize plans for an attack on Washington, DC. Based on Webster's intelligence, Union troops stormed the meeting and rounded up the conspirators at gunpoint before they could carry out their plans against the federal capital. A few of the society members were intentionally allowed to escape in the ensuing confusion. One of them was Webster.

Webster continued his spying. Now the Southern government asked him to carry messages to Confederate spies in the North and return with their replies. Webster gladly took on the mission. He opened and read all the communications he got from the Confederates and reported everything to Pinkerton before delivering the messages to their intended recipients. He also revealed to Pinkerton the names of Confederate spies in Washington, DC.

No one in the South ever suspected Webster of working for the Union. But his luck ran out when the spy became ill with inflammatory rheumatism in February

1862. The illness made it impossible for him to travel and he could neither deliver his messages nor contact Pinkerton. He was stuck in Richmond with no way to communicate his exact whereabouts to the North.

Worried, Pinkerton sent two agents south in March to try to find Webster. They went to Virginia first and tracked Webster to Richmond. But the two men, John Scully and Pryce Lewis, were quickly recognized in the Confederate capital as Northern spies.

DYNAMIC DUO

Webster did not always work alone. Hattie Lawton, who also worked for Pinkerton, accompanied Webster on several of his missions behind enemy lines in the South. She posed as Webster's wife, but she was also working as a spy, collecting information about Confederate troops and war plans. When Webster became ill with inflammatory rheumatism in Richmond in 1862, Lawton stayed by his side and gave him medical attention. She was arrested with Webster, tried, and found guilty of spying. She was sentenced to one year in prison. After her release, Lawton reported back to Pinkerton in 1863 and then disappeared, never to be heard from again.

They were pointed out by several people who had been detained in Washington, DC, in 1861 as Confederate spies, and then allowed to move to Richmond. The two operatives were part of the team that had investigated and questioned the suspected Confederate spies.

Scully and Lewis were taken into custody. After a quick trial, they were given a death sentence. To save his own life, Scully revealed that Webster was a spy. Based on the information Scully provided, Webster was arrested and sentenced to death. Scully and Lewis were both released.

PRYCE LEWIS
1832–1911

Before walking into trouble searching for Timothy Webster in March 1862, Pryce Lewis had distinguished himself as an exceptional operative for Allan Pinkerton.

Born in Wales in 1832, Lewis came to New York City in 1856 and became a traveling salesman with a publishing house. But in 1859 he moved to Chicago, where he took a job as a grocery clerk. Looking for a life of adventure, he ran into an old acquaintance who worked as a detective with Pinkerton and decided to give that job a try.

He was taught how to investigate cases, shadow suspects, use disguises, and assume a persona, talents he drew on extensively during the Civil War. Using his British accent to his advantage, Lewis posed as either a British aristocrat or a wealthy merchant, interested in buying Southern cotton. Based on information Lewis received, the Union army seized control of the Kanawha Valley in western Virginia on July 24, 1861. The Union gained a foothold in the area that the North never relinquished throughout the course of the war. That victory came only three days after the First Battle of Bull Run and gave the beleaguered Union a major boost.

Pinkerton and President Lincoln both threatened the South that if Webster were executed, the North would execute a Southern spy in retaliation. Up to that point in the war, neither side had carried out a death sentence on any spy. Instead, spies were used in prisoner exchanges.

The Confederates were not fazed by the Union threats. In addition, they were embarrassed by how easily they had been duped by the Union spy. Webster's death sentence was carried out on April 29, 1862. He was the first spy to be executed in the Civil War. Pinkerton said of Webster, "No braver nor truer man died during the War of the Rebellion than Timothy Webster."[1]

Despite Northern threats, Union officials did not immediately execute any Confederate spies in their custody. But, starting in 1863, the Union did hang a number of convicted Confederate spies.

PHILIP HENSON: DIVIDED LOYALTY

Philip Henson was such a good double agent that even his wife, Celestine, was not quite sure which side he was on. Celestine knew her husband was involved in the war, but she did not know what he did.

When the Civil War broke out in 1861, Philip Henson was 34 years old. A Southerner who was born in Alabama and lived part of his adult life in Mississippi, Henson was against secession. He favored the North but had friends in the South. He helped both sides in the war, but he gave a little extra to the North. Henson served as a spy for generals on both sides. He was likable, easygoing, and knew the Mississippi territory extremely well.

Henson began spying for the North in late 1862, when Union forces, led by General Ulysses S. Grant, entered Mississippi. Union intelligence officers asked him to be a spy after he helped the federal army secure some much-needed supplies when they entered Mississippi. He was sent on a mission to get information on Southern troops in Columbus, Mississippi. When he arrived in Columbus, Confederate troops surrounded him and took him to see General Daniel Ruggles.

The Confederates suspected Henson was a spy. Cool and calm, Henson mentioned names of people he knew in the area. He also gave Ruggles some information about Union troop movements a short distance away from Columbus. Ruggles was impressed, and he not only released Henson but gave him a paying job as a scout for the Confederates. For a short time, Henson was actually a paid employee of both the North and the South.

UNSTOPPABLE

Philip Henson lived on the edge for the entire war. He was captured by the Confederates in late 1864 and imprisoned as a spy. Henson always claimed to be innocent. To prove it, Henson asked to be released so he could serve in the Twenty-Sixth Mississippi Regiment. Desperate for troops at that point, the Confederates released him, but they sent guards with him on a train to make sure he joined his unit. While on the moving train, Henson jumped off and made his way back to Union lines. Union general Grenville Dodge said of Henson, "He was probably one of the best—if not the best—men we ever had in our employ."[2]

One of Henson's boldest missions came as Grant was planning to attack the Confederate stronghold of Vicksburg, Mississippi, in the spring of 1863. Union general Grenville Dodge, Grant's spymaster, asked Henson to go to Vicksburg and gather as much information as he could about the Confederate forces there. Using contacts he had in the city, Henson got through the Confederate lines and set up a meeting with Southern general John C. Pemberton.

Pemberton commanded the Southern forces in Vicksburg. Henson told Pemberton about the harsh treatment Southern prisoners of war were getting at

As spymaster for Grant, Dodge developed an efficient spy network capable of gathering information from many places.

VICKSBURG

After a long siege that started on May 18, 1863, the Union Army of the Tennessee, led by Ulysses S. Grant, finally took Vicksburg on July 4, 1863. The intelligence gathered by double agent Philip Henson figured prominently in this Northern victory. The capture of Vicksburg was extremely significant for the North. It gave the Union control of the Mississippi River, split the South in two, and isolated many parts of the Confederacy, including Texas, Louisiana, and Arkansas. Those Confederate states were blocked by the Union army from sending troops and supplies to aid Southern troops in the East. After Vicksburg fell, the Union had a stranglehold on the Confederacy.

the hands of the Union. The general was impressed with the information Henson gave him. He asked Henson to talk to all the Confederate troops in Vicksburg and tell them about these horrid conditions. Pemberton believed the tales of mistreatment of Southern war prisoners would rally his troops and make them better fighters.

To accomplish this task, Henson was given access to the entire city of Vicksburg. After getting all the intelligence he needed and speaking to all the Southern troops, Henson headed back to the Union lines. Before he left, Pemberton congratulated the double agent on the great job he did to inspire Confederate troops. When Henson gave the information he gathered to General Dodge, the Union spymaster said it was "of incalculable benefit to us."[3]

Harriet Tubman used the many connections she made helping slaves escape in the 1850s and early 1860s to develop an extensive spy network during the Civil War.

BOLD, DARING, AND COURAGEOUS

Every one of the spies in the Civil War was beyond courageous. They also brought to their task steely determination and a deep commitment to gathering vital information that would help their side win the war.

Even if she had not been a spy, nobody could ever question Harriet Tubman's bravery. Born a slave in 1822 on Maryland's eastern shore, Tubman escaped slavery in 1849, fleeing to Philadelphia. For the next 11 years Tubman made many trips to the South, rescuing hundreds of slaves. Tubman would become the most famous conductor on the Underground Railroad. She was known by the code name Moses, after the biblical figure who freed the Israelites from slavery in Egypt.

During the Civil War, Tubman aided the North, first as a cook and nurse, then as a spy. She worked in South Carolina alongside Union general David Hunter and Colonel James Montgomery. Part of her job was to organize a spy network and meet behind enemy lines with African Americans who gave her information about the Confederate military. Tubman put her life at great risk. The Confederates had a reward out for her capture because of the work she was doing with the Underground Railroad. She also led military raids.

In the early-morning hours of June 2, 1863, Tubman, along with Montgomery, led a group of federal soldiers in gunboats up the Combahee River in South Carolina on a mission to free slaves and destroy several plantations. By raiding and destroying cotton plantations, the main source of income in the South, the Union hoped to inflict economic hardship on

THE UNDERGROUND RAILROAD

The Underground Railroad began in the early 1800s. It reached its peak in the 1850s and 1860s. The term *Underground Railroad* referred to a network of people, meeting places, safe houses, and routes used to help slaves in the South escape to freedom in Northern states and Canada. By 1850 more than 100,000 slaves had escaped bondage through the efforts of the Underground Railroad.[1] The railroad was organized by small groups of antislavery activists, including white abolitionists, Quakers, freeborn African Africans, former slaves, and Native Americans. Underground Railroad conductors, who led slaves to safety, relied heavily on solid intelligence to get the job done. The Underground Railroad, then, served as an ideal training ground to prepare Harriet Tubman for her work as a Union spy during the Civil War.

The success of the Combahee River Raid struck a strong blow to the Confederacy, which depended on the area for supplies.

the South. But the Confederates had prepared for a Northern assault. Southern troops had planted mines in the river to blow up unsuspecting enemy ships that traveled the Combahee. Tubman, however, had learned about the mines from her spy network and managed to guide the ships around the mines. As the boats arrived on the Carolina shore, the Union troops saw some slaves Tubman's operatives had already gathered. Then the troops moved inland, freeing more slaves and burning plantations and cotton fields. Roughly 750 slaves were rescued that night and brought north.[2] Tubman was the only woman known to have led a military raid in the Civil War.

BELLE BOYD: "SIREN OF THE SHENANDOAH"

The South had a secret weapon early in the war in a feisty, rebellious 17-year-old woman from Martinsburg, Virginia, named Belle Boyd. Boyd was furious when a group of Union soldiers came to her home on July 4, 1861, to investigate reports she had Confederate flags displayed in her room. Federal troops were occupying Martinsburg at the time. When the troops arrived, one of them cursed at Boyd's mother and shoved her aside. Outraged, Boyd responded by taking out a pistol and killing the soldier. "I could stand it no longer; my indignation was aroused beyond control. . . . I drew my pistol and shot him," Boyd later recalled.[3] An inquiry was conducted into the shooting and the federal government decided not to press charges. That decision only emboldened the young woman.

The Union army decided to put guards around the Boyd home to keep an eye on the family. The young spy befriended some of the guards and got them to boast to her about their knowledge of the Union army plans for the region.

Belle Boyd, a notorious Confederate spy, had several nicknames, including Siren of the South, Siren of the Shenandoah, and Rebel Joan of Arc.

Through couriers, she forwarded that information to Confederate troops who were trying to regain control of Martinsburg and the surrounding area.

In the spring of 1862, Boyd went to visit her aunt in Front Royal, Virginia, in the Shenandoah Valley. She was distressed to learn the Union army had taken over her aunt's small hotel.

But she used that to her advantage. While living at the hotel, she realized that the Union war council held meetings in the hotel parlor. In a bedroom right above the parlor, there was a small hole in the floor of the bedroom closet. Through that hole, Boyd heard everything that was said during the war council meetings. She memorized the details and, when the meetings ended, rushed to write down what she had heard. She then passed her detailed notes along to Confederate commanders once again, using couriers loyal to the South.

During one Union war council meeting in mid-May 1862, Boyd heard Union general James Shields would be changing positions, moving east of Front Royal and leaving the town with a reduced number of Union troops. Boyd knew Southern general Thomas "Stonewall" Jackson was in the middle of an ongoing campaign to gain control of the Shenandoah Valley. Jackson's relentless push in the Shenandoah Valley had started in the spring of 1862.

With the information she gained through eavesdropping on the Union war council, Boyd jumped on her horse, rode 15 miles (24 km) in darkness, and got

SHENANDOAH VALLEY CAMPAIGN, 1862

Boyd and several other Confederate spies supplied key information to Confederate general Jackson, which helped him conduct one of the most brilliant military campaigns in the Civil War. Outnumbered and outgunned, Jackson led his men hundreds of miles along the strategic Shenandoah Valley in Virginia from March to June 1862. First, he fought five important and challenging battles. Jackson was able to corner much larger Union forces and outmaneuvered them. He also confused Union military leaders and forced them to continually change their war plans. Finally, Jackson pressured the Union defenses in nearby Washington, DC, and prevented the Union from capturing the Confederate capital of Richmond early in the war. With each victory, Jackson's legend grew, along with the morale of Confederate forces.

the information to Jackson. The Confederate general launched an attack on Front Royal on May 23, easily beating back the diminished Union force.

As the battle raged, Boyd learned the outnumbered Union soldiers were planning to burn bridges in the area to stop Jackson's troops from chasing after them. Dodging bullets, Boyd brought news of the Union plan to Jackson. The general sent his troops to the bridges in time to stop the destruction. When the battle in Front Royal ended, Jackson sent Boyd a personal note of thanks. Her exploits were covered by newspapers in both the North and the South, and they earned her the nickname the "Siren of the Shenandoah."[4]

GEORGE ELLSWORTH: MASTER WIRETAPPER

George Ellsworth used a different method than Boyd's to find out about Union war strategy. Ellsworth was a master wiretapper, an unusual talent for the time. He rode with the Second Kentucky Cavalry under the command of the notorious guerrilla-style fighter General John Hunt Morgan. Early on, they fought mostly in Kentucky and Tennessee, then they moved into southern Indiana and Ohio later in the war.

A telegraph operator by trade, Ellsworth could easily listen in on Union messages being sent between different Northern commanders. As a result, he and Morgan always knew where the Union army was going to be and what it was planning.

But Ellsworth's work went further than that. Morgan and Ellsworth devised a plan to have the telegraph operator send misleading messages over the telegraph lines to Union troops. Those messages caused great confusion among Union forces. The befuddled federal troops never knew where they should be or when to advance. The Confederates made the most of the chaos they created, beating back unprepared and baffled Union fighters at every turn.

PAULINE CUSHMAN: ACTRESS EXTRAORDINAIRE

Most spies have to be good actors. They play a role and must be convincing enough to get the enemy to trust them with sensitive information. Pauline

Actress and Union spy Pauline Cushman posed for a photo in a soldier's uniform after receiving the honorary title of major.

MAJOR DEVELOPMENT

President Lincoln and the Union army brass were very impressed with Pauline Cushman's bravery. After the Union army rescued her from Confederate forces in Shelbyville, she was given the honorary military title of major by Union generals Gordon Granger and James A. Garfield. Cushman continued to aid the Union army after her rescue, but she could no longer work as a spy. Her identity had been compromised in her last mission. However, because of the extended tour she had done with her show through Tennessee, Kentucky, Alabama, and Mississippi, she knew the terrain well. That information allowed the Union army to draw accurate maps of the region. Cushman remained on the stage after the war and was billed as "Major Cushman."[5]

Cushman, an actress by profession, viewed spying as a way to serve her country in the Civil War.

Born in Louisiana in 1833 but raised in Michigan, she was fiercely loyal to the Union. In 1863, she was touring with a show in the South, visiting Mississippi, Tennessee, and Kentucky. In April of that year, she met with Union colonel Orlando H. Moore, the head of military police in Louisville, Kentucky. Cushman was performing at the town theater in Louisville. She reported several Confederates asked her to declare her support for the Confederacy while onstage. The thought outraged her. But Moore had an ingenious idea. He believed such a declaration would convince Southern sympathizers in Kentucky that Cushman was a loyal Confederate and take her into their confidence.

The actress jumped at the opportunity to play the part. So one night, after her show was over, she publicly praised Confederate president Davis. The plan worked just as Moore thought it would. Before long, Cushman was quite popular among Confederates throughout Kentucky. They were telling her about everything from guerrilla raids to dates and times of supply shipments. Cushman reported it all back to the Union army, along with lists of Confederate spies in Kentucky and neighboring Tennessee.

She continued her work as a Union spy until early June 1863, when she was captured by the Confederates in Shelbyville, Tennessee. The Southern troops caught Cushman with Confederate war plans hidden in her shoe. Found guilty of spying in a hastily arranged military trial, she was sentenced to hang shortly after her arrest. Using her exceptional acting talents, she faked an illness. That delayed the Southern military from carrying out the sentence long enough for Cushman to be saved by the Union army. On June 27, 1863, Union troops staged a daring rescue of Cushman and captured Shelbyville.

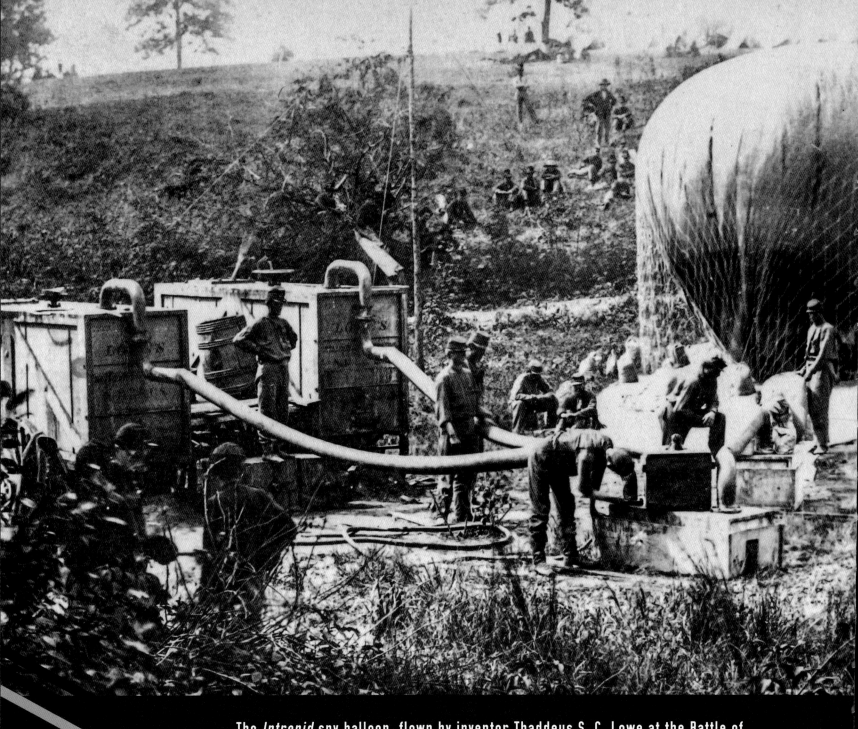

The *Intrepid* spy balloon, flown by inventor Thaddeus S. C. Lowe at the Battle of Fair Oaks in Virginia, was one of many tools of spycraft used in the Civil War.

CHAPTER

8

★ ★

SPYCRAFT

From the earliest days of espionage, spies have used a variety of tools to carry out their missions. One of those tools was a disguise kit, to make sure no one, even by chance, recognized them and blew their cover. These disguises have ranged from wearing eye patches and changing hair color to wearing wigs and growing beards and mustaches. Spies also used tools such as invisible ink, codes, ciphers, and binoculars to help pass secret messages along or gather information from afar. These important tools of the trade made the spy's job much easier.

SARAH EMMA EDMONDS: "PRIVATE FRANKLIN THOMPSON"

Union spy Sarah Emma Edmonds was hardly ever out of disguise. Edmonds wanted to fight for the North in the war, but women were not allowed to serve in the military. So Edmonds cut her hair, put on men's clothing, and assumed the identity of a man by the name of Franklin Thompson. In April 1861, Thompson enlisted in the Union army as a member of the Second Michigan Infantry. After

UP IN THE AIR

Aerial reconnaissance and surveillance played a role in the Civil War as spying went airborne. Both Union and Confederate forces used large hot-air and hydrogen balloons to spy on each other from the air, but not for long.

The balloons had a capacity of approximately 15,000 cubic feet (425 cu m) of air or hydrogen. The Union army used them occasionally between 1861 and 1863. The Confederate army, which only used the balloons in 1862, had difficulty making them because the materials needed for the balloons were expensive and hard to get in the South.

Each balloon had a woven basket suspended below it for aeronauts to stand in and conduct surveillance. The aerial marvels floated across the sky and tracked troop movements, especially during battles. However, the balloons were at the mercy of the wind and could easily be carried miles off course.

Although they were considered useful tools for spying and intelligence gathering, the technology was ultimately discarded because the balloons violated a very basic rule of espionage: They were visible.[1]

some training, Edmonds, alias "Private Thompson," was assigned the job of a male nurse in the Army of the Potomac, fighting in Virginia.

After the capture of Union operative Timothy Webster in April 1862, the North was looking for a spy to replace him. Private Thompson volunteered for the dangerous task. Having successfully disguised herself to get into the army, Edmonds had numerous ideas for disguises she could use to cross enemy lines and gather valuable intelligence to help the Union win the war.

On her first mission to Yorktown in April 1862, she used silver nitrate to darken her skin and pretended to

Sarah Emma Edmonds dressed as an African-American contraband, one of many disguises she took on during the war.

be a male slave. She infiltrated a Confederate camp and was put to work with other slaves. She roamed around the camp, doing her work and overhearing Confederate troops openly discussing the South's next moves in the war. She slipped out of the camp as easily as she had come in, and she reported back to the Union command, then led by General McClellan.

Union commanders sent her out on more missions. She disguised herself according to the character she believed would most likely accomplish each mission. Edmonds played an African-American maid, an Irish peddler with a perfect Irish accent, and, on many occasions, a Southern belle. All the Northern brass knew was that Private Thompson got the job done.

JOHN SCOBELL: ASSUMING DIFFERENT PERSONAS

John Scobell, an African-American spy who worked for spymaster Allan Pinkerton, was another spy who took on different personas. Scobell played a variety of roles, all with precision. He posed as a butler, a cook, a peddler, a bartender, a laborer, a servant, an entertainer, and a deckhand, to name only a few.

Scobell had been a slave in Mississippi, where his master taught him to read, write, and play a banjo, all talents that came in handy when Scobell was freed in July 1861. The former slave headed north, where he got a job with Pinkerton. He was the detective's first African-American operative.

At first Scobell was given the assignment to roam the Virginia countryside as a lighthearted minstrel who was heading back to his plantation. He offered to entertain homesick Confederate troops with his banjo tunes. In reality, he was noting troop locations and movements while also hoping to overhear any war plans. The soldiers often spoke freely in front of Scobell, believing he was uneducated and did not understand what they were talking about. The spy gathered some vital information, and his detailed reports impressed Pinkerton.

As an African American, Scobell got into places most agents could not because he did not arouse suspicion when he served food and drinks to Confederate officers or worked in the fields around military camps. In these undercover roles, the hardworking spy listened, observed, and gleaned a great deal of intelligence useful to the Union.

In early 1862, Scobell, now a skilled spy, was sent to Richmond to work with Pinkerton agent Hattie Lawton, who was masquerading as a Southern socialite at

THE POCKET TELEGRAPH

A pocket telegraph was small enough to fit in a pants pocket, but it was one of spying's biggest tools. The pocket telegraph was invented to help repair telegraph lines. It consisted of a telegraph key to tap out the message and a sounder to produce the audible sound.

People who repaired telegraph lines used the device to determine where a problem was along the telegraph line. Spies, however, used the pocket telegraph to intercept messages. All a spy had to do was climb a telegraph pole and attach a wire between the line and the pocket telegraph. The spy could then intercept every message sent along that line.

the time. Scobell pretended to be Lawton's servant. The pair visited Southern fortifications throughout Richmond. Lawton, an attractive woman who was approximately 35 years old, created a distraction. She flirted and chatted with the Confederate officers. Meanwhile, Scobell slipped away unnoticed to inventory the supplies in the forts and sketch entrenchments. All this information was sent north for Pinkerton to share with General McClellan.

SPECIAL TOOLS

Spies such as Edmonds and Scobell used a variety of tools to help them do their jobs. One of those tools was invisible ink. Anything mildly acidic, including lemon juice, grapefruit juice, or even milk, could be used as invisible ink. The acid weakened the fibers in the paper. When the paper was held near a source of heat, the weakened fibers darkened first and the message appeared.

An alternative to invisible ink was writing a message in code or cipher. However, both the sender and the recipient had to know the code or cipher. The various spymasters, generals, and operatives in the war had different codes and ciphers. Codes and ciphers are not the same. A code is a system of letters of the alphabet, numbers, words, symbols, or signals used to communicate something other than what they seem to mean. For instance, the code word for Union spy Harriet Tubman was *Moses*.

6	r	n	b	h	b	x
3	v	1	w	8	4	w
1	e	m	3	y	5	g
5	l	a	9	o	i	d

Elizabeth Van Lew carried this written code with her in her watch case until she died in 1900.

A cipher is a way to keep words or messages secret by rearranging letters of the alphabet. Sometimes numbers are part of the cipher as well. Those who use a particular cipher make it up, so a cipher is often difficult to figure out or, in spy terms, to crack. There is no standard cipher. For instance, spymaster Elizabeth Van Lew created her own cipher system, which she shared with only a few Union officers.

A cipher disk, or wheel, helps with enciphering and deciphering a cipher. In the Civil War, cipher wheels were approximately 2.25 to 4 inches (5.5 to 10 cm) in diameter.[2] The cipher wheel had an outer circle and an inner circle. The inner circle turned and lined up with the letters or numbers on the outer circle.

To send a message, the sender and the recipient both had to have identical wheels. There are two key letters that are used to set the wheel. For instance, the letter C on the outer wheel might line up with the letter W on the inner wheel. Once the two circles are identically aligned, the enciphered message can be deciphered.

Spies during the Civil War sometimes had to observe their targets from afar. By the 1850s, binoculars, or field glasses, were very popular. When the war broke out, these "spy glasses" came in very handy. This latest tool for enhancing vision allowed operatives to see what they needed when getting up close was too dangerous.

LESSONS LEARNED

Although intelligence gathered by spies frequently had a profound effect on the course of the war, few if any spies were recognized for their work. For spies in

Binoculars were an indispensible tool for spies during the Civil War.

the Civil War, there was no glory on the battlefield. Most worked in anonymity, keeping their identities secret for their own safety and effectiveness. Their heroics, bravery, and sacrifices were known to only a few.

Spies in the conflict were a diverse group. In this role that encouraged both deception and trust, spies from varied backgrounds made valuable contributions to both sides. During the Civil War, the practice of having every commander working with his own team of spies and various government agencies running individual espionage networks resulted in confusion and needless duplication of effort.

OFF TRACK

Railroads came of age during the Civil War. The effect of rail lines was enormous, giving both sides a fast, practical, efficient way to move troops, food, weapons, and other supplies. Naturally, railroads became the target of spies. Knowing when supplies and troops were on the move was valuable information. It gave enemy troops an opportunity to slow down or even sabotage rail activity.

Samuel Ruth was the superintendent for the Richmond, Fredericksburg and Potomac (RFP) Railroad, a vital supply line for the Confederates. Unbeknownst to the South, Ruth was a Union loyalist and a spy for the North. Ruth often slowed down RFP shipments so they reached their destination too late to be useful. He also kept the Union informed about movements of Confederate troops and supplies by rail.

The Civil War ended on April 9, 1865, with Lee's surrender to Grant at Appomattox Court House, Virginia. After the war, a conflict-weary nation disbanded the Army of the Potomac's Bureau of Military Information. With the war over, spying was viewed as divisive and spies themselves as less than honorable. Spying was considered an obstacle to healing the nation. It was not until 1882 that the US Navy founded the Office of Naval Intelligence, the first permanent centralized federal intelligence agency in the country. The Office of Naval Intelligence was designed to spy exclusively on foreign military operations. The US Army established its own centralized military intelligence division in 1885. Both units were extremely valuable to the nation in the Spanish-American War (1898).

Espionage conducted during the Civil War paved the way for these intelligence units and other agencies that followed, including those still in operation, such as the Central Intelligence Agency. Operatives in today's US intelligence community still walk in the footsteps of the Civil War spies. These daring operatives laid the foundation for modern spy tactics.

PICTURE PERFECT
A SPY TOOL IN DISGUISE

By the time the Civil War broke out, photography was becoming very popular throughout the United States. Newspapers had not yet developed the technology to print photos. However, battlefield photographs were used as the basis for newspaper illustrations of the war and were considered the forerunners of American photojournalism.

For Civil War spies, carrying a camera, though a bit clunky-looking, was considered one of their best disguises. Some of those who shot photos on the battlefield also used their cameras as tools for intelligence gathering. Alexander Gardner, a photographer in Washington, DC, joined forces with Pinkerton and the Union army in 1861. At first Gardner photographed terrain so mapmakers could come up with accurate maps. Then, so that Northern commanders might detect possible spies in their ranks, Gardner was supposedly asked to take group photos of Union military units. Anyone a commander did not recognize in the photos was questioned. The plan worked so well that Confederate spies were warned never to pose for photos.

Photography was also used for espionage. Andrew David Lytle was a photographer for the Confederacy. He went from one Union camp to another, seemingly taking photos of the troops. Although he appeared to be a wandering photographer trying to earn a living, he was reportedly a Confederate spy tasked with photographing Union artillery, troop formations, supply wagons, and military leaders.

TIMELINE

November 6, 1860
Abraham Lincoln is elected US president.

February 23, 1861
An assassination attempt on Lincoln is foiled by Allan Pinkerton's operatives.

March 4, 1861
Lincoln is sworn in as president.

April 12, 1861
The American Civil War begins with the Confederate firing on Fort Sumter in Charleston Harbor in South Carolina.

April 29, 1862
Timothy Webster is the first spy to be executed in the Civil War.

May 23, 1862
Confederate spy Belle Boyd provides information that helps lead to a Confederate victory in the Battle of Front Royal.

August 30, 1862
The South wins the Second Battle of Bull Run.

June 2, 1863
Union spy Harriet Tubman leads the successful Combahee River Raid.

June 8, 1861

Lincoln's call for troops prompts additional Southern states to secede from the Union.

July 21, 1861

The South wins the First Battle of Bull Run, aided by information from Southern spy Rose O'Neal Greenhow.

August 23, 1861

Pinkerton arrests Greenhow as a spy.

March 9, 1862

The battle of the ironclads, the *Monitor* and the *Virginia*, ends in a draw.

June 27, 1863

The Union army rescues spy Pauline Cushman right before her execution.

July 1–3, 1863

The North wins the Battle of Gettysburg, thanks in part to information from Union spy Charlie Wright.

July 4, 1863

Union general Ulysses S. Grant captures Vicksburg, Mississippi.

April 9, 1865

The Civil War ends.

ESSENTIAL FACTS

KEY PLAYERS

- A private detective, Allan Pinkerton organized the Union's first spy and counterintelligence network.

- A socialite spy operating out of Washington, DC, Rose O'Neal Greenhow became the spymaster of one of the South's most successful spy rings.

- An exceptional double agent, Timothy Webster was one of the Union's greatest spies.

KEY EVENTS

- Detective Allan Pinkerton and his operatives foiled a plot by Southern secessionists to assassinate Abraham Lincoln before his inauguration in early 1861.

- Rose O'Neal Greenhow and her network of Southern spies provided key information to General P. G. T. Beauregard, which enabled the Confederacy to win the First Battle of Bull Run on July 21, 1861.

- The spying efforts of young Belle Boyd helped Confederate general Thomas "Stonewall" Jackson win a decisive victory in the Shenandoah Valley campaign in the spring of 1862.

- Elizabeth Van Lew created an important Northern spy network in 1861 that supplied the Union army with valuable intelligence throughout the war. She also placed an African-American spy in the Confederate White House.

- African Americans offered the North vital intelligence on Confederate troop movements and war plans throughout the Civil War. Their reports were known as "black dispatches."

IMPACT ON WAR

The Civil War taught military leaders on both sides that superior spies are as valuable as superior weapons. Destroying the enemy is the purpose of a superior weapon. Finding out where and when to strike with that weapon is the mission of a superior spy. That mission takes courage, commitment, and coordination. The bravery of those involved in spying during the Civil War was unmatched, their commitment unwavering. However, the overall spying operations on both sides lacked centralized control. The lessons learned from not having that kind of centralized approach to information gathering gave way to today's centralized intelligence agencies.

QUOTE

"I employed every capacity with which God has endowed me, and the result was far more successful than my hopes could have flattered me to expect."

—Rose O'Neal Greenhow

GLOSSARY

ABOLITIONIST

A person who wants to end slavery.

CIPHER

A code or disguised way of writing.

CONTRABAND

A slave who, during the Civil War, escaped or was brought within Union lines.

COVER

The assumed identity of a spy.

GUERRILLA

A fighter who uses irregular methods, such as sabotage or surprise raids, against a larger force.

INFILTRATE

To gain access to a place or organization gradually in order to obtain secret information.

MILITIA

A military force made up of nonprofessional fighters.

MINSTREL
A traveling performer. Minstrel shows in the United States in the 1800s often used crude racial stereotypes for humor.

ONSLAUGHT
A military attack or offensive.

RECONNAISSANCE
An exploration of an area to gather information about the activity of military forces.

SECESSION
The formal withdrawal of one group or region from a political union.

SKIRMISH
A minor battle between two groups of enemy troops.

SURVEILLANCE
Close observation or watch kept over something or someone.

TOPOGRAPHY
The arrangement of physical features of a landscape, including mountains, hills, and rivers.

ADDITIONAL RESOURCES

SELECTED BIBLIOGRAPHY

Abbott, Karen. *Liar Temptress Soldier Spy: Four Women Undercover in the Civil War*. New York: HarperCollins, 2014. Print.

Bonansinga, Jay. *Pinkerton's War: The Civil War's Greatest Spy and the Birth of the U.S. Secret Service*. Guilford, CT: Lyons, 2012. Print.

Jones, Wilmer L. *Behind Enemy Lines: Civil War Spies, Raiders, and Guerrillas*. Dallas, TX: Taylor, 2001. Print.

FURTHER READINGS

Allen, Thomas B. *Harriet Tubman, Secret Agent: How Daring Slaves and Free Blacks Spied for the Union during the Civil War*. Washington, DC: National Geographic, 2006. Print.

Cummings, Judy Dodge. *Civil War*. Minneapolis: Abdo Publishing, 2014. Print.

Jarrow, Gail. *Lincoln's Flying Spies: Thaddeus Lowe and the Civil War Balloon Corps*. Honesdale, PA: Calkins Creek, 2010. Print.

WEBSITES

To learn more about Essential Library of the Civil War, visit **booklinks.abdopublishing.com**. These links are routinely monitored and updated to provide the most current information available.

PLACES TO VISIT

International Spy Museum
800 F Street Northwest
Washington, DC 20004
202-393-7798
http://www.spymuseum.org
This museum is dedicated to exploring the craft, practice, and history of spying. It often hosts lectures and exhibits on Civil War spying, and its website contains information about Civil War spies and spycraft.

National Cryptologic Museum
8290 Colony Seven Road
Annapolis Junction, MD 20701
301-688-5849
https://www.nsa.gov/about/cryptologic_heritage/museum
This museum traces the history of sending and reading secret messages using ciphers and codes, especially during wartime.

SOURCE NOTES

CHAPTER 1. SAVING LINCOLN

1. Jay Bonansinga. *Pinkerton's War: The Civil War's Greatest Spy and the Birth of the U.S. Secret Service.* Guilford, CT: Lyons, 2012. Print. 46.

2. Ibid. 57.

3. Allan Pinkerton. *The Spy of the Rebellion: History of the Spy System of the United States Army during the Late Rebellion.* New York: G. W. Carleton, 1883. Google Books. 85.

4. Jay Bonansinga. *Pinkerton's War: The Civil War's Greatest Spy and the Birth of the U.S. Secret Service.* Guilford, CT: Lyons, 2012. Print. 114.

5. Ibid. 124.

CHAPTER 2. IN PLAIN SIGHT

1. Michael Golay. *Civil War*, updated ed. New York: Facts on File, 2003. Print. 32.

2. Michael J. Sulick. *Spying in America: Espionage from the Revolutionary War to the Dawn of the Cold War.* Washington, DC: Georgetown UP, 2012. Print. 81.

3. Rose Greenhow. *My Imprisonment and the First Year of Abolition Rule at Washington.* London: Richard Bentley, 1863. *Google Books.* 18.

4. Harnett T. Kane. *Spies for the Blue and Gray.* Garden City, NY: Doubleday & Company, Inc., 1954. Print. 36.

5. Rose Greenhow. *My Imprisonment and the First Year of Abolition Rule at Washington.* London: Richard Bentley, 1863. *Google Books.* 193.

CHAPTER 3. SPYING BY THE MILITARY

1. Jay Bonansinga. *Pinkerton's War: The Civil War's Greatest Spy and the Birth of the U.S. Secret Service.* Guilford, CT: Lyons, 2012. Print. 163.

2. Wilmer L. Jones. *Behind Enemy Lines: Civil War Spies, Raiders, and Guerrillas.* Dallas, TX: Taylor, 2001. Print. 29.

CHAPTER 4. SPY RINGS

1. Elizabeth R. Varon. *Southern Lady, Yankee Spy: The True Story of Elizabeth Van Lew, a Union Agent in the Heart of the Confederacy.* New York: Oxford UP, 2003. Print. 48–49.

2. Wilmer L. Jones. *Behind Enemy Lines: Civil War Spies, Raiders, and Guerrillas.* Dallas, TX: Taylor, 2001. Print. 49.

3. Jay Robert Nash. *Spies: A Narrative Encyclopedia of Dirty Deeds and Double Dealing from Biblical Times to Today.* New York: M. Evans, 1997. Print. 489–491.

SOURCE NOTES
CONTINUED

CHAPTER 5. BLACK DISPATCHES

1. Michael Fellman. *The Making of Robert E. Lee*. Baltimore, MD: Johns Hopkins UP, 2000. Print. 201.

2. Donald E. Markle. *Spies & Spymasters of the Civil War*. New York: Hippocrene, 1994. Print. 61.

CHAPTER 6. DOUBLE AGENTS

1. Liz Stern. "Part IV: The History behind the Pinkertonian Mystery." *History Detectives*, New York Historical Society Museum & Library, 7 July 2012. Web. 25 Feb. 2016.

2. Donald E. Markle. *Spies & Spymasters of the Civil War*. New York: Hippocrene, 1994. Print. 128.

3. Ibid. 129.

CHAPTER 7. BOLD, DARING, AND COURAGEOUS

1. "What Was the Underground Railroad?" *Harriet Tubman Historical Society*. Harriet Tubman Historical Society, n.d. Web. 28 Dec. 2015.

2. Beverly Lowry. *Harriet Tubman: Imagining a Life*. New York: Doubleday, 2007. Print. 318.

3. "Belle Boyd." *American Civil War Story*. American Civil War Story, n.d. Web. 25 Feb. 2016.

4. Ibid.

5. Ferdinand Sarmiento. *Life of Pauline Cushman: The Celebrated Union Spy and Scout*. New York: United States Book Company, n.d. Print. 846.

CHAPTER 8. SPYCRAFT

1. "Intelligence throughout History: The Birth of Overhead Reconnaissance." *News and Information*. Central Intelligence Agency, 3 June 2011. Web. 25 Feb. 2016.

2. Mark C. Hageman. "The Cipher Disk 'Signalling in Cipher.'" *Signal Corps Association*. Signal Corps Association, n.d. Web. 29 Jan. 2016.

INDEX

ABOUT THE AUTHOR

Robert Grayson is an award-winning former daily newspaper reporter and the author of books for young adults. Throughout his journalism career, Grayson has written stories on historic events, sports figures, arts and entertainment, business, and pets. These stories have appeared in national and regional publications, including the *New York Yankees* magazine and *NBA Hoop*. He has written books about the Industrial Revolution, the American Revolution, the California Gold Rush, animals in the military, and animal performers, as well as the environment, law enforcement, and professional sports.